Animals in the Wild

Lizard

c2

by Vincent Serventy

Raintree Publishers
Milwaukee

Snakes and lizards are the most common reptiles in the world. This knob-tailed gecko from Australia is just a few inches long. Other lizards grow ten feet long.

Geckos are among the few lizards that make
sounds. The barking gecko sounds like a small
dog. This one is shedding its skin, or molting.
All lizards shed their skin as they grow.

Like most reptiles, chameleons have scaly skin.
Most chameleons live in Africa and Madagascar.
They hide from enemies by changing their
color and blending into the background.

The chameleon has large eyes that swivel.
They can see in many directions. When a
chameleon spots an insect, it flicks out
its long, sticky tongue to catch it.

The world's biggest lizard is the Komodo
monitor, also called the Komodo dragon. Some
grow ten feet long and weigh 300 pounds.

Komodo dragons catch and eat goats, deer,
water buffalo, wild pigs, and even people.
They live on the islands of Indonesia.

The perentie is the largest Australian lizard. It eats a variety of foods, including smaller lizards and snakes. It uses its long, forked tongue to smell animals as it hunts for food.

There are many kinds of monitor lizards. They are found in Asia, India, and Africa. In Australia, they are called goannas. This perentie monitor grows about seven feet long.

This sand monitor is almost as big as a
perentie. It lives in sandy areas and digs

a hole for shelter during the winter. It uses its long, sharp claws for climbing trees.

The tree monitor lives in wooded areas. It
climbs trees to look for eggs and baby birds.
On the ground, it eats young rabbits and foxes.

The sharp spines of the thorny devil serve the same purpose as a porcupine's quills. They protect this mother and baby from enemies.

Iguanas are found in North and South America, in Madagascar, and in Fiji and Tonga. This rare green-banded iguana from Fiji eats fruit, leaves, and flowers, as well as insects.

Marine iguanas of the Galapagos Islands are the
only lizards that feed in the sea. They dive
into the water to eat seaweed. But they come
up on land to breathe air, as all reptiles do.

Dragon lizards have bodies covered with sharp,
pointed scales. When scared, this bearded
dragon of Australia spreads out the spiky scales
under its chin. The frilled dragon on the cover
shows an umbrella of skin to scare its enemies.

The flying dragon lives in Asia and Indonesia.
It has flaps of skin on either side of its body.
When it spreads out these flaps, it can glide
from tree to tree. When it climbs a tree, it folds
the flaps back against its body.

Skinks live all over the world. Their bodies
are usually smooth, but their shapes vary.
This copper-tailed skink is eating a beetle.

This is a blue-tongued skink with its newborn
babies. Some lizards are born alive, and some
are hatched from eggs.

Most of the smaller skinks eat insects. The
bigger skinks eat plants. This Australian
skink scares away enemies by opening its pink
mouth and sticking out its blue tongue.

The European fence lizard is brown when it is young but turns green as it grows older.
Many lizards, like the one in the picture, break off part of their tails to escape from enemies.

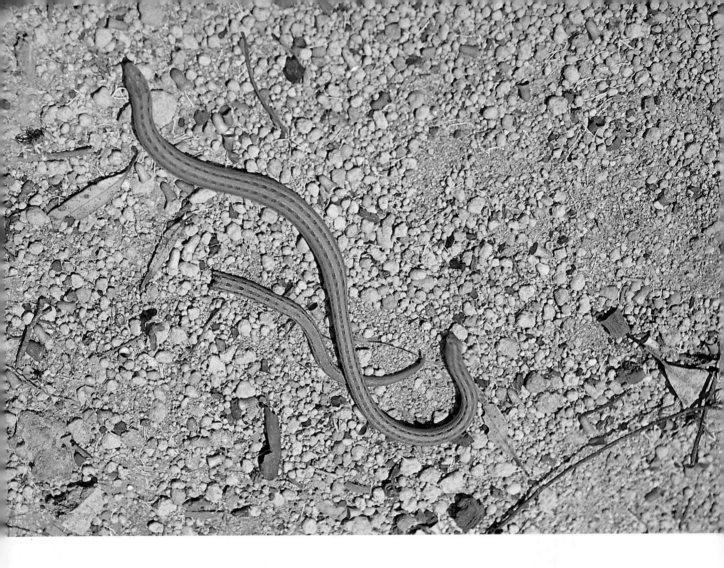

Some lizards look like snakes because their legs are so tiny. This snake lizard has been frightened and has broken off its tail. When the enemy grabs the wriggling tail, the lizard can escape. It then grows a new tail.

Only two lizards have a poisonous bite. They are the Gila monster of the United States and the beaded lizard of Mexico. But most lizards are helpful to people because they eat insects which damage farmers' crops.

First published in the United States of America 1986
by Raintree Publishers, 310 West Wisconsin Avenue,
Milwaukee, Wisconsin 53203.

Reprinted in 1989

Library of Congress Number 86-17835

First published in Australia in 1985 by
John Ferguson Pty. Ltd.
100 Kippax Street
Surry Hills, NSW 2010

The North American hardcover edition published by arrangement
with Gareth Stevens Inc.

Text and illustrations in this form copyright© Vincent Serventy 1985

Acknowledgments are due to Vincent Serventy for all photographs in
this book except the following:
Gunther Schmida: front cover; Jane Burton, Bruce Coleman Ltd: p 4, p
21; Kim Taylor, Bruce Coleman Ltd: p 5; Fritz Vollmar, Bruce Coleman
Ltd: p 15; Rod Williams, Bruce Coleman Ltd: p. 23.

ISBN 0-8172-2706-7 (U.S.A.)

Library of Congress Cataloging in Publication Data

Serventy, Vincent.
  Lizard.

  (Animals in the wild)
  Summary: Depicts various kinds of lizards in their natural
surroundings.
  1. Lizards—Juvenile literature.   (1. Lizards)
I. Title. II. Series.
QL666.L2S47 1986   597.95   86-17835
ISBN 0-8172-2706-7 (lib. bdg.)

2 3 4 5 6 7 8 9 10 11 12 13   99 98 97 96 95 94 93 92 91 90 89